Gift Baskets

for All Seasons

75 Fun and Easy Crafts Projects

Gift Baskets

for All Seasons

75 Fun and Easy Crafts Projects

Elizabeth Jane Lloyd

ABBEVILLE PRESS · PUBLISHERS · NEW YORK · LONDON · PARIS

First published in 1997 by HarperCollins*Publishers* London

First published in the United States of America in 1996 by Abbeville Press,
488 Madison Avenue, New York, N.Y. 10022.

Text written by Lucy Peel
All photography by Sue Atkinson

First edition
1 3 5 7 9 10 8 6 4 2

ISBN 0-7892-0295-6

Contents

MAKING THE MOST OF BASKETS

Of all the items in common use by households across the globe, baskets must be among the most enduring. They provide an unbroken link that can be traced back as far as the times of such lost civilizations as those of the ancient Greeks and the Romans. The flimsy remains of baskets have also been discovered in the tombs of ancient Egyptians, and it is reasonable to assume that they were being used by our ancestors centuries before that.

Baskets were originally designed purely for everyday use, for such humble tasks as storing utensils or food, and for fetching and carrying. Their widely varying styles, which we find so attractive today, grew out of practical need, their shapes evolving according to the particular use they were going to be put to. Baskets for loaves, for example, needed to be long and shallow, while baskets for storing rice or cooking paraphernalia needed to be narrow and deep.

Over the centuries, these basically mundane household objects took on entirely different roles. People began to recognize them as objects of beauty in their own right and to realize their potential for many uses other than those for which they were originally intended. And so they were pressed into many other roles, from the everyday—such as storing newspapers—to the fun, as receptacles for pretty flower arrangements, for pinecones, dried grasses and seedheads, or even for Christmas baubles.

We are lucky today in that we have a veritable United Nations of baskets available to us, imported from all over the world. So while our own country's baskets may be both attractive and beautifully made, we can still satisfy our desire for the unusual: after all, it is always fun to try something different.

Baskets are constructed from natural materials, whether it be willow, rush, rattan or plywood. As we become more aware of our threatened environment, this becomes a definite plus. We are happy to use something entirely natural, especially if it means banishing nonbiodegradable plastic containers to the rubbish heap of history.

Every household will have a basket or two somewhere, whether it is in day-to-day use or sitting forgotten in a corner. If yours are hidden away, now is the time to brush off the dust and turn your basket into something truly splendid, worthy of a prime position in your home, with the help and inspiration of the ideas contained in this book.

The glory of this is that it is so simple. There is no need to trek off to the store and spend a lot of money on equipment: instead, whatever you have to hand can be pressed into use either to decorate or else to fill your baskets. The key is improvisation. It is astonishing how something as plain and utilitarian as a shopping basket can be dressed up, with the help of a few ribbons or strands of ivy, to look unusual and special, worthy of being filled with something appealing.

Odd scraps of material can be pressed into use to make a basic lining for an old basket, and suddenly you have a work basket to be proud of. The flower arranger's basic tool, oasis, is indispensable in a basket: with it you can easily create a wonderful centerpiece for a dining table

or, if you are using a hanging basket, a flowering display to decorate a summer supper on the terrace.

Let the children get in on the act when creating brimming baskets: they will have hours of amusement decorating eggs for Easter, making fruit or figures out of bread dough, or cooking a multinational collection of gingerbread people, dressed in their national costumes. A basket filled with such delights becomes a work of art in itself—and will be sure to lend flair to a children's party.

Naturally, the time of year will dictate what materials are available to fill your decorative baskets, and the projects in this book are divided into different seasons. Spring offers a wide variety of new bulbs, while summer brings a profusion of colorful blooms. In autumn, richly hued gourds, or golden-colored dried seedheads and grasses, can take the place of flowers and look just as spectacular—and will last a lot longer. Winter also provides a wealth of material to fill baskets, from Christmas candles or baubles to potted plants like poinsettias or the early flowering, sweet-scented hyacinths or narcissi.

Some of the best fun can be had with *objets trouvés*, such as shells collected on a vacation at the seaside, or interesting feathers picked up on a walk through the woods. Everything can be put to good use.

Nothing except the limits of your imagination will stop you making the best use of baskets. Hopefully, this book will give you inspiration and ideas enough to push those limits to their full extent.

SPRING

When the first daffodils raise their bright heads to the pale blue of an early spring sky, we know that winter is finally over. St. Valentine's Day beckons in the early spring season; then there is Easter to prepare for. Easter is a particularly enjoyable festival, having none of the pressures of Christmas, yet just as many opportunities for fun.

Spring brings with it a host of cheerful bulbs, many of which will look wonderful in a basket. Simply pot them up in a shallow inner container, or line the basket with plastic first and plant the bulbs in it directly. This is a perfect way to bring a little bit of spring sunshine indoors: the bright colors of flowering bulbs will thoroughly dispel the gloom of winter.

SPRING PANSIES

Of all the so-called common flowers, the little pansy must be one of the sweetest. With its jolly nodding head and open face, it is the optimist of the flower world. It is always cheerful-looking and always bright—in colors as well as outlook.

This unassuming little plant is, nevertheless, one of the most popular among gardeners. And rightly so, for among its many varieties it is always possible to find one to bloom at a particular time of year. Pansies also come in every color of the rainbow, which is extremely useful for anyone designing with flowers.

These numerous different shades and color combinations illustrate perfectly how skillful nature is at contrasting as well as mixing and matching different colors and shades—such as deep rich purple and vivid yellow.

Wicker basket of pansies

Cheerful pansies and twining ivy have been planted in compost to create this brimming spring basket (*right*). The basket is lined with plastic first.

Putting on ivy and pressed flowers

Ivy is ideal for decorating a basket as it lasts a long time without water and has strong, flexible stems that can be threaded easily through the wide gaps in the basket work. Pansies, however, do not have this endurance, so dried, pressed pansies are the only option. If pressed carefully (*see page 16*) they will keep their color and shape, and their delicate, papery-fine petals will provide an attractive contrast to the fresh living flowers. The pansies are wired to attach them to the basket.

WIRING THE PRESSED PANSIES

1. Once the flower has been pressed, take approximately 15cm (6in) of fine florist's wire and very gently push it through the base of the flower head under the petals.
2. Fold the tip of the wire into a U shape with one end shorter than the other. Coil this short end around the stub of the stem and the rest of the wire.
3. Thread the wire through the sides of the basket and twist around the ivy stems to secure both.

Pressing flowers

One of the great joys of this craft is that there is no need to buy expensive equipment. Even a flower press is not necessary, since any good, thick book—a weighed-down telephone directory is ideal—will do the job just as well. Be sure to close the book carefully to avoid damaging your specimens. The best method is gently to roll the pages closed.

Pressing flowers and foliage is also extremely easy. All you have to do is leave the plants in their press or book for six weeks in a dry, airy place, checking once for mildew, and then they are ready. The results will look beautiful mounted on velvet or silk, as well as on different colors and types of paper. They can be made into pictures, bookmarks or even, more ambitiously, set in resin as paperweights.

Choose only perfect specimens for drying

Best of the bunch

Be very choosy when picking your flowers. Discard anything not perfect and collect them early in their season, soon after they have bloomed, as their color is at its best then.

Blotting paper will absorb the moisture

Heavy book for weighing down

Pressed pansies
Pansies are among the easiest flowers to press, being flat and open to start with. Their vivid colors also make them good subjects for pressing and they are pretty enough to be mounted alone.

Making posies
As long ago as the Middle Ages posies made up of herbs (also known as tussie mussies) were carried, like a pomander, to ward off disease and foul smells. By the nineteenth century posies had become a vital fashion accessory, to be carried by women on social occasions—such as visits to the opera or dances. A rose would normally be placed at the center of the posy, with the whole arrangement being held upright in porcelain, silver, or enamel posy holders.

For a natural-looking posy, pansies—with their jolly, open faces and bright colors—are ideal flowers. Simply wrap a few pansies in a twist of thick colored paper, set them off with a ring of ivy, and finish with a silky ribbon. Choose contrasting paper for a dramatic look, or a matching shade for a gentler effect. Silver-colored aluminum foil makes a good alternative.

Freshly picked pansies

Bright silk ribbon

Bright silver foil adds contrast and sets off the posy

Thick colored paper

BE MY VALENTINE

February marks the start of longer days and the first tentative signs of spring, such as the hardier shoots pushing their way out of the ground and a few brave buds preparing to burst open. It is a time of weak sunshine and of broad optimism, as the long winter finally seems to be on the wane.

February the fourteenth, the feast of St. Valentine, was when birds were traditionally said to pair off, so what better day to send a love token to a sweetheart? The custom of exchanging such tokens, usually anonymously, dates back as far as the eighteenth century, when it was said that, on that day, the first person of the opposite sex you laid eyes on was destined to be your Valentine.

Those unwilling to leave so much to chance might content themselves with the Victorian custom of sending cards on Valentine's Day, although there are other traditional gifts. Chocolates are frequently given as a romantic offering and are now available in heart shapes too. Why not give a basket filled with small chocolate hearts and embellish it with doves, as shown (*left*)?

Red roses—with the red representing passion and the heart and the thorns representing the painful course of true love—are another archetypal token. A single rose was always thought the most romantic, while now, with the availability of cheaper imported blooms (particularly the aptly named *Rosa* 'Only Love'), a dozen is usually considered the magic number.

VALENTINE'S BASKET

For something a little more imaginative than a plain bouquet, a basket of roses (*right*) is ideal. To make a truly memorable present for someone you love, surround the roses with a halo of the dainty gypsophila, sometimes known as baby's breath, and complete the arrangement with a shiny frill of crinkly red cellophane. Here the cellophane has been given a pretty zigzag edging with a pair of pinking shears.

All-year-round Valentine
For the truly romantic, love tokens need not be confined to Valentine's Day. All-year-round gifts with a love message are easy to make and always appreciated. A heart-shaped basket bursting with the bounty of the season is attractive as well as delicious.

Sprigs of bay leaves threaded through the wickerwork

Cherries attached to basket

Tasty soft fruits

Sculptural globe artichoke

Shallow basket in the shape of a heart

Tender new potatoes and peas

Petits fours

The name *petits fours* is French for little oven. However, some of these showy little delicacies are not baked at all and are more like confectionery than cakes.

Petits fours look wonderful made of marzipan, which can be molded into all sorts of pretty shapes and unusual colors.

Marzipan, also called *marchpane*, is an Arab recipe and was brought to Europe by the Moors. It is very malleable, so can be used almost like a modeling clay to be molded or sculpted into a variety of shapes.

Marzipan

450g/1lb ground almonds
450g/1lb confectioners' sugar
grated rind of a lemon
2 eggs, beaten
makes about 1kg/2lb

1. Mix the almonds, sugar, and lemon rind.
2. Slowly add the eggs, stirring with a fork.
3. As the mixture becomes moist, mix by hand.
4. Once all the egg has been added, knead the mixture into a smooth paste.

If these shapes will be eaten, you could buy premade marzipan which does not use raw eggs. To dye marzipan, add a few drops of food coloring and knead well to coat evenly. To create a frosted effect, sprinkle the coated petits fours with icing sugar.

To make the roses above, mold small balls of marzipan into little petals. Cut the tiny flowers decorating the hearts with a metal cookie cutter.

GINGERBREAD

The warm, spicy taste of ginger combined with the crumbly biscuit pastry is a glorious taste sensation, equally suitable for an adult spring picnic or a children's party. Gingerbread has a variety of associations. What child, or adult for that matter, does not know the story of Hansel and Gretel, the wicked witch and her gingerbread house, or the little gingerbread man running as fast, fast, fast as he can? Maybe because of all these fairy stories and folk tales, there is a tendency to associate gingerbread with Eastern Europe; however, ginger —which is one of the most versatile and widely used spices of all—is popular throughout the world.

Making gingerbread is fun, and so easy that it will keep children happy for a couple of hours on a wet afternoon—particularly since there is the prospect of a delicious treat once it is cooked.

The added advantage is that gingerbread actually improves by being kept for a couple of days, wrapped in foil or in an airtight container, before it is eaten. It can therefore be made in advance for any special event, such as a birthday party. A basket filled with homemade gingerbread makes a lovely gift. Try to choose an unusual basket— something slightly ethnic and rustic would be ideal—and "dress" your assortment of gingerbread people in their appropriate national costumes.

Gingerbread can be cut into any number of shapes, using ready-made cookie cutters. They can be used to make pretty decorations to hang from your Christmas tree, for example, or even to make love tokens, such as these two hearts (*above*). To make a hole through which to thread a length of ribbon for hanging, use a drinking straw to pierce the hole, *before* the dough is baked.

BASKET OF GINGERGBREAD
This trough-shaped basket is filled with an assorted family of gingerbread people, their jolly faces and attractive costumes created with piped icing and colored candies.

Gingerbread

Gingerbread

175g/6oz butter or margarine
175g/6oz brown sugar
2 eggs, beaten
450g/1lb plain flour
1-2 teaspoons ground ginger
2 teaspoons ground mixed spice

Dressing up
Experiment with jokey "costumes," such as Miss World (*far right*) or even portraits—in the loosest sense—of your children and their friends. Children love these, and they will be a welcome addition to any party bag when it comes to going-home time.

Preheat the oven to 180°C/350°F.

1. Cream butter and sugar together until light and fluffy. Gradually add eggs until combined.

2. Add the spices to the flour, then gradually add dry ingredients to the butter mixture.

3. Turn dough out onto a smooth surface and knead lightly. Wrap in plastic wrap and chill for 30 minutes.

4. Roll out the dough, a quarter at a time, between two sheets of baking parchment or waxed paper to about 1cm (½in) thickness.

5. Remove top sheet of paper and cut out shapes, using a cookie cutter. Remove the waste.

6. Transfer the parchment to a cookie sheet and bake each batch for 10-15 minutes.

7. Decorate when cool with piped icing (dyed with food coloring) and candies.

Gingerbread

A family of nations
A traditional basket, such as this magenta Mexican basket, filled with a jolly assortment of festive gingerbread people, would make a wonderful feature sitting in the middle of a children's birthday-party table.

Piped icing is used to create features

Colorful ethnic basket

Brightly colored candies add decoration

EASTER EGGS

Decorated Easter eggs are often associated with Eastern Europe and the Pysanka folk-art eggs (made using a wax-resist method) of Russia, Poland and the Ukraine.

Czechoslovakia also has a strong tradition, with the eggs being painted rather than dyed, and the Germans and Dutch create beautiful eggs with intricate decorative detail. In fact German settlers introduced this art to America and even today the tradition continues, with egg-decorated trees or branches being popular at Easter in many parts of the United States.

Yet the art of egg decoration is actually centuries old. In ancient Greece, Rome and Egypt, eggs represented rebirth and so were symbols of spring. Because of this and their scarcity, eggs were valued highly and were greatly appreciated as gifts. But they were not given to be eaten—instead they were decorated and made to be treasured for years.

As the centuries passed, the popularity of egg decorating spread throughout the world, and the the decoration became ever more elaborate and extravagant as time advanced. By the thirteenth century, members of the king's household in England were given eggs covered in gold leaf. This excessive opulence reached its zenith in Russia at the time of the last czar, with the exquisite creations of the jeweller Peter Carl Fabergé, who made eggs from crystal and precious metals encrusted with jewels.

While the association of eggs with Easter dates back to classical times, it was only in this century that the habit of giving chocolate eggs became so widespread—before that, chocolate was a great luxury and prohibitively expensive. However tasty chocolate eggs may be, they are still rather impersonal: it is so much nicer to give someone an egg you have decorated yourself.

EASTER OFFERINGS

A simple basket filled with gaily decorated eggs makes a wonderful gift or centerpiece at Easter. For a truly authentic touch, place the eggs on a bed of dark green watercress—an Eastern European tradition.

Tall-handled
wicker basket

Guinea fowl
feathers

Attaching feathers

Feathers add a dramatic finishing touch to a
basket of eggs, their fluffy softness contrasting
beautifully with the hard, smooth surface of the
eggs. They are easy to attach to the basket: just
thread the quill between the wicker strands and
secure with a fine piece of florist's wire.

Decorative
speckled
quail eggs

Soft downy
feathers

BLOWING EGGS

Before you dye or decorate your egg, you will need to empty it. Have the egg at room temperature—if too cold it will be hard to blow.

1. With a large pin (a hatpin is ideal), pierce both ends of the egg, making a small hole at the pointed end and a slightly larger one at the bottom.

2. Gently rotate the tip of a sharp pair of scissors in the larger hole to enlarge it to 5mm (¼ in).

3. With the pin, jiggle around inside the egg through the larger hole to pierce the membrane; this will enable the egg to be blown.

4. Hold the egg over a bowl and blow through the small hole, forcing the contents out of the larger hole.

5. Rinse out the egg, prop it up on paper and allow it to dry.

DYEING EGGS

Commercial dyes are available in craft shops and they are suitable for dyeing eggs. However, it is fun to make your own natural dyes. Spinach produces a lovely green, carrots an orangey-red, and even coffee grounds can be used to create a rich brown. But some of the best colors—from a wonderful maroon to a reddish-brown—can be obtained from onion skins.

1. Place skins in a saucepan of cold water and bring to the boil, then reduce the heat and leave to simmer for an hour.

2. Remove the dye from the heat and allow to cool before straining off the skins.

3. Place the eggs in the pan, ensuring they are filled with liquid dye to prevent them floating.

4. Return the pan to the stove and heat to boiling, before reducing to simmering point. Leave until the eggs are dyed to the required shade, then rinse in cool water and allow to dry.

USING A FELT-TIP PEN

Use a permanent felt-tip pen to create folk art eggs by outlining a painted design or, as here, drawing simple patterns onto a dyed egg.

1. Sketch the design on to a dyed egg with a pencil.

2. Draw over the pencil guide marks with your pen—the thickness of the line will determine the delicacy of your design.

3. Spray with a fixative to seal the pattern.

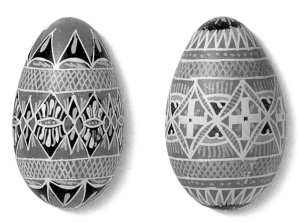

Intricately painted designs on dyed eggs

FERN-WRAPPED EGGS

You can use all sorts of natural materials to create beautiful designs. Small flat flowers, such as daisies, buttercups and violets, work well, as do small leaves. But for a truly delicate, elegant pattern a small frond of fern cannot be beaten.

1. Take a pair of pantyhose and cut across the legs at intervals to make tubes.
2. Lay the fern face down flat against the egg and slide into one of the tubes, then gather the ends of the tube and pull taut so the fern is held firmly against the egg. Tie the ends firmly.
3. Dye following the method outlined on page 29, then carefully peel off the tube and the fern to reveal the design.
4. Spray on a fixative.

RESIST-AND-SCRATCH DESIGNS

Eastern Europeans use wax to create this effect in a method called Pysanka. There is also a simpler method of scratch carving called *sgraffito.*

1. Lightly sketch your design onto a dyed egg.
2. Using anything sharp-tipped—a nail, scalpel or tip of a very pointed pair of scissors—gently scratch away at the shell over your pencil marks until the undersurface shows through.
3. Spray with a polymer-medium fixative—gloss or matte—for a professional-looking finish.

Three different ways of attaching ribbon

ATTACHING RIBBON

A pretty, brightly colored ribbon is more than a means of simply suspending an egg. It will add a new dimension to any design. Here are a few simple methods of attaching a ribbon.

1. Tie or glue a thin ribbon to the center of a short matchstick and slide the end of the matchstick into the larger hole in the egg. The stick will wedge itself crossways in the egg, holding the ribbon firmly.
2. Tie a knot in thin ribbon, then thread it through the eye of a long darning needle. Push the needle up through the egg, then unthread.
3. Fold a long length of narrow ribbon in half and tie the ends together. Bend one end of a piece of fine florists' wire into a long U-shape. Push this through the top egg hole and out through the bottom one, then hook the looped end of the ribbon over it. Pull the wire back through the egg, taking the ribbon with it. Knot the ribbon at the top of the egg, either leaving the loop or snipping one end to leave a single strand. You may fold the ribbon back down over the egg to tie at the bottom.

Flower-wrapped design *Resist-and-scratch design* *Fern-wrapped design*

Easter egg basket
The coiled raffia basket
is filled with a collection of
simply and elaborately decorated
eggs, showing the rich variety
of this folk art.

SUMMER

The profusion of flowers in the summer is overwhelming and quite glorious. Take advantage of the wonderful variety to fill baskets and jugs for inside the house as well as outdoors. A beautiful arrangement cascading out of a hanging basket in the garden, or a spectacular display in a tall storage basket indoors, will make a dramatic focal point and convey the full glory of the summer season while being positively life-enhancing in its beauty.

FLOWER BASKETS

In summer we are spoiled for choice with the variety of blooms available. This is the time of year when the weather allows us to fling open all the windows and bring the garden into the house. Similarly, the abundance of blooms makes it so easy and tempting just to pick or buy a bunch of flowers and pop them in a vase without much thought. Of course they will look pretty, but it is so much more satisfying to go to a little extra effort and end up with something truly spectacular.

Baskets look particularly good brimming with flowers. Always take care when matching the basket to your flowers. Natural, meadow or woodland flowers look wonderful tumbling out of a rustic-style basket but would be lost in anything too formal, while more sophisticated blooms demand something really special. Try filling a basket with flowers to match the furnishings and color in a room of the house, or even to suit a particular occasion or mood. Flowers have a language of their own, so an arrangement can be designed to convey an appropriate message. For example, the flower girl at a wedding could hold a basket of roses, symbolizing love, combined with something evergreen, representing life everlasting, or maybe honeysuckle, which stands for devotion. Children bearing baskets of flowers have in fact played an important role in festivals throughout Europe for centuries. May Day processions, for example, would not have been complete without an entourage of little flower girls bearing blossom-filled baskets.

BASKET OF HOT COLORS
Provided the basket is simple, an arrangement of cut flowers can be placed outdoors to provide a valuable focal point. The attractive fountain shape of the arrangement (*right*) was achieved with the help of florist's foam, which can hold stems in place even at these angles. The rich purple of the lizianthus combines with the bright colors of the asters and gerberas, set off by their halo of eucalyptus.

Everlasting flower basket

Silk, with its delicate texture and beautiful sheen, lends itself well to imitating the shapes and habits of different flowers. In fact a carefully chosen and arranged bouquet of silk blooms, as here, can be just as attractive as the real thing. This suspended wire basket, with its extravagant curlicues, is an excellent choice for such an opulent collection of artificial flowers. Sited near a window, it can be appreciated from both indoors and out and it will retain its beauty until you tire of the arrangement and wish to replace it with something else.

Candlelit basket

To light a summer evening's supper party in the garden, suspend above your table a hanging basket filled with moss and plants and surrounded by a trio of candles (*left*). The combination of the flickering flames, the delicate trailing tendrils of foliage and the gently nodding heads of the flowers (in this case convolvulus) looks enchanting and will guarantee that your party is remembered as a magical occasion.

DISGUISING THE CHAINS

Hide the ugly chains used to suspend hanging baskets by winding ribbon or silky gift-wrapping tape around them (*right*).

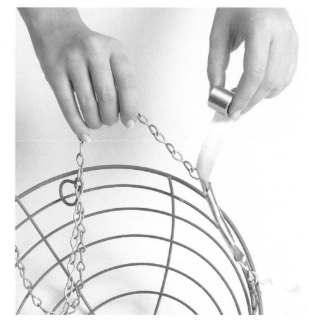

USING OASIS

Water-retaining florist's foam, known as oasis, has transformed the art of flower arranging. Prior to its appearance in the 1960s, a whole variety of materials, mainly wire, had to be used to hold flower stems in place.

Foam works particularly well when used with bushy plants or in conjunction with moss, which will hide both it and any ugly stalks. Before use, submerge the foam in water for about 20 minutes until it is soaked right through (place a weight on the foam initially to keep it from floating). Cut it to size using a craft knife or other sharp knife. Then simply push the stems of cut flowers into the oasis. Keep it topped up with water daily.

Try mixing cut and growing plants in a basket arrangement. For this basket, vividly colored cut alstromeira lilies held in oasis have been combined with glossy green palms and other small indoor plants to create a sophisticated contemporary look.

POT-ET-FLEURS

The practice of combining cut flowers and growing plants in the same arrangement is called pot-et-fleurs. The joy of this method is that a permanent, evergreen framework can be transformed according to the choice of cut flowers added to it. It is also a clever way of spicing up any dull existing plantings.

Simply sink small, slim containers, such as yogurt cups, to hold the cut flowers into the potting mix around the growing plant, or arrange the flowers in oasis (as shown here), before filling up the basket with mix for the living plants.

Flower basket with bells

Combining hard and soft objects, such as these substantial bells and a collection of delicate-looking flowers, can be extremely effective. The spiky thistles, in particular, make a wonderful contrast to the rounded smooth metal, while the gentle curves of the irises, the bright colors of the asters and the rough wickerwork of the basket add interest.

POPPIES

Wild flowers such as poppies, cornflowers, cowslips and grasses have been collected and arranged in informal bunches for centuries. Together with cornflowers and daisies, poppies were often seen as the weeds of traditional cornfields—yet it was these plants that were traditionally gathered to celebrate good harvests.

Poppies have several other associations too. The poppy motif, often entwined with ivy, appeared repeatedly in the Art Nouveau movement. This movement—with its organic lines and curling tendrils—was influential in persuading many people to reevaluate their concept of beauty in plant terms.

At the end of the First World War the battlefields in France, where thousands of soldiers were horribly slaughtered, became smothered in scarlet poppies. And so the flowers that created these carpets of brilliant red became potent symbols of remembrance and consolation. Yet the poppy, with its peculiar, almost papery petals and sooty black center, is above all a cheerful flower.

While fresh, living poppies are extremely beautiful, these flowers have the ability to delight even when dead. Dried poppy seedheads are wonderfully sculptural and have many uses in dried flower arrangements. Shake out the tiny black seeds and save them to scatter on a bare patch of earth in the garden, then enjoy the amazingly rich pattern of barklike textures the seedheads make when they are massed together.

BASKET OF SUMMER FRUITS

Arrange small bunches of dried poppy seedheads informally around the rim of a basket and fill it with an assortment of ripe soft fruits. The rich red of the cherries and strawberries and the glossiness of their skins contrasts wonderfully here with the brittleness of the dried poppies, while recalling their glory when alive. If you can find some strawberries with foliage attached you will really have a spectacular offering with which to impress guests at the end of a lazy summer lunch.

Fresh and dried poppies
Never dismiss poppies as weeds. They may grow wild in profusion, but their good looks and brilliant colors mean they can hold their own against the most sophisticated cut flowers. As they are relatively short-lived, however, try drying the seedheads for a completely different effect.

Poppy seedheads
Fresh poppies, with their delicate papery petals, are transformed into woody-looking seedheads when dried. Gathered into small bunches, they are interesting enough to be displayed on their own, but for a really spectacular effect bind them up with silky ribbon or stand them in an unusual basket.

Freshly picked poppies

Bunch of dried poppy seedheads

MAKING A POPPY SEEDHEAD WREATH
Simple to make, this looks delightful hanging in the kitchen or above a fireplace. For an average-sized wreath you will need about 150 seedheads, 3m (10ft) of ribbon and some fine florist's wire.

1. Cut the poppy stems to approximately the same length.
2. Gather the seedheads into small bunches (*see left*) and bind together with wire.
3. Arrange the seedheads so that they are evenly distributed along the bunch.
4. Bind the bunches together, using wire and ribbon simultaneously, to form a circle.

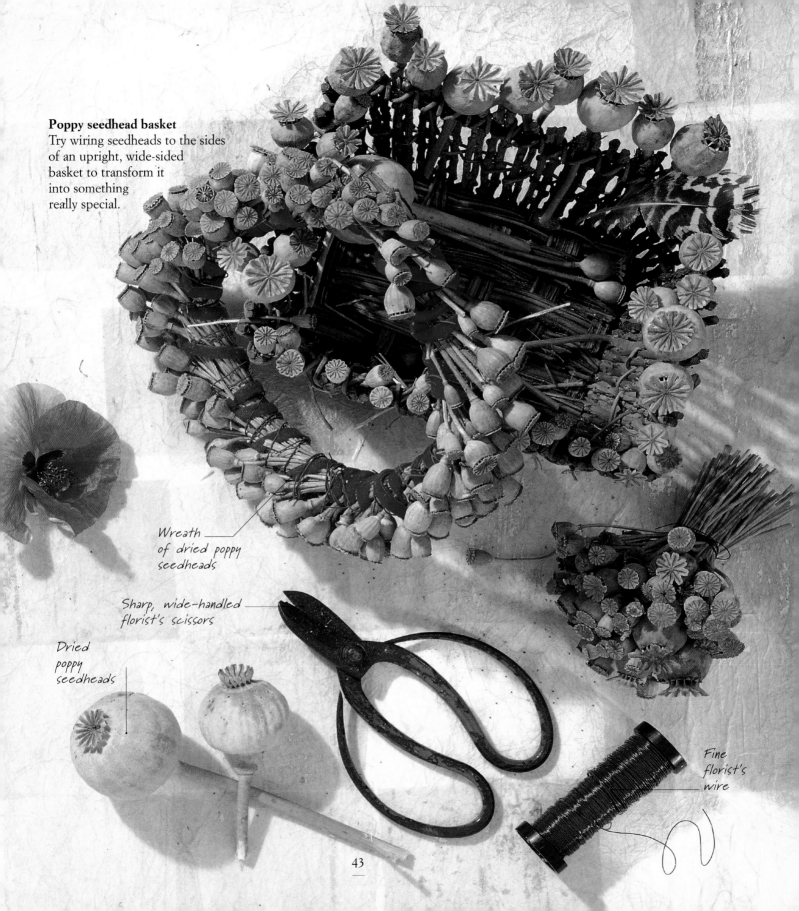

Poppy seedhead basket
Try wiring seedheads to the sides
of an upright, wide-sided
basket to transform it
into something
really special.

Wreath
of dried poppy
seedheads

Sharp, wide-handled
florist's scissors

Dried
poppy
seedheads

Fine
florist's
wire

Shaker basket of poppy seedheads

The pure line and simplicity of the Shaker basket (*left*) dramatically offsets the richness and intricacy of the seedheads, while its lovely rich brown color complements their lighter, subtle shades.

The Shaker influence

The Shakers are an American religious sect whose members live in communities practicing celibacy and praising God with vigorous dancing—hence their name. They make exquisitely simple objects—their tall ladderback chair being possibly the best known—as a form of living prayer or offering to God. These circular baskets, made in a series of diminishing sizes, are another example of Shaker craftsmanship: their beauty lies in their form and the unadorned use of richly colored wood. Shaker designs are now very much in vogue.

Poppy eye, containing thousands of dark spores

Distinctive papery red petal

Weed-like stems

Small bud

The poppy symbol

In the language of flowers, red poppies stand for consolation, in part due to their association with the First World War.

DRYING AND USING POPPY HEADS

Once you have collected your seedheads, gather them into small bunches and gently shake out the seeds over a sheet of paper. Hang the bunches upside down in an airy place to prevent the stalks drooping as they dry. Scatter the seeds over a patch of earth for a splash of color later on.

PICNIC BASKETS

Among most people's favorite recollections of childhood, there is sure to be a happy memory of a picnic. Just think of a hot, sunny summer's day and the joy of seeing a blanket covered with delicious goodies. Picnics are wonderful family outings, with great excitement for the children and surprises for the adults, but they can also be extremely romantic occasions.

While it is fun just to throw a few bits and pieces together and set off on the spur of the moment, it is also very enjoyable planning a picnic in advance and working out a theme of some kind—maybe one that fits the setting.

Themed picnics

Having a special theme works particularly well with children, who usually need something more than attractive scenery and good food to keep them happy for several hours. A few toys, some novelty food and the opportunity to make something that can then be saved as a keepsake never goes amiss.

A picnic beside a river or lake is wonderful on a hot day, as even the proximity to water is somehow cooling, and there is always plenty to see and do by the water side, from observing small fish or skimming pebbles in the water from a riverbank to watching boats ply up and down on a lake or canal. So if you have a child's birthday, or another special occasion to celebrate, why not try a boating theme?

RIVERSIDE BIRTHDAY PICNIC

For a feast sure to delight children, take an old mushroom or fruit basket and fill it to bursting with chunks of ham, small sausages and tomatoes all stuck on cocktail sticks, which in turn are stuck into an orange or a grapefruit. Don't forget the vital lemonade, lollipops, and some chocolate goodies. To make it really special, add balloons, toy boats to float and liquorice-allsorts necklaces (which the children can make themselves). No one could possibly be bored on this picnic.

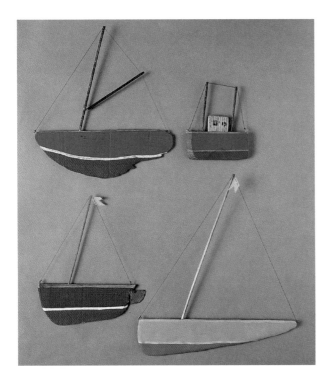

Driftwood boats

These small boats (*left*) look beautiful above a child's bed and will be a constant reminder of happy summer days.

MAKING THE BOATS

Driftwood boats can easily be made from flotsam washed up on the shore or from odd pieces of wood. Paint the wood, stick on a twig mast, then attach screweyes through which to thread string for rigging. Use scraps of fabric for sails.

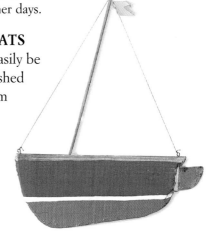

Romantic picnic for two

Formal and impromptu picnics are both fun, but mix in a little romance and they cannot fail to be a success (*left*). A delicious *al fresco* meal can be made to look quite elegant. Simply pack an ordinary willow basket with edible treats and a bottle of wine or champagne, then add a red ribbon as a final flourish. Food always tastes delicious outdoors and a feast of olives (and olive bread), grilled Cornish game hens, French cheeses, delicious fresh fruit and chocolates will satisfy even the most jaded palate. For such a sumptuous spread only champagne will do, and a proper tablecloth to cover your picnic blanket. To complete the splendid picture of elegance and romance, place a red rose in a vase in the center of your feast.

THREADING LIQUORICE ALLSORTS

Liquorice allsorts are as colorful as the prettiest beads, and strung together they make jolly, as well as tasty, necklaces. Use a thick needle and heavy thread to string the sweets, then tie the ends tightly.

SHELL
BASKETS

Collecting shells need not be a hobby exclusive to children; in fact the gentle joys of beachcombing must make it one of the few pastimes guaranteed to appeal to young and old alike. Surprisingly it need not be confined to the summer, as a walk along a beach in winter, with the waves crashing dramatically on the shore, can be just as enjoyable—and as productive—as an amble along the shoreline at low tide under a warming summer sun. It is also worth looking out for interestingly shaped pieces of driftwood and the sun-bleached skulls of seabirds.

While our seas may not yield the large, exotic shells found in the tropics, they can still provide a wonderful selection in many sizes and colors. In the eighteenth and nineteenth centuries, shells were often displayed in collectors' cabinets, made into pictures or used to adorn frames and boxes. Today they are more likely to be arranged in a basket, where they form a fascinating collection of *objets trouvés*.

If you are not fortunate enough to have been to the seaside recently, or are short of shells, you could try visiting your local supermarket, as they may be willing to give you some scallop shells if they have them. Or you can buy a big bag of mussels, which are relatively cheap and are quite delicious to eat. Their dark shells can look most attractive glued on to the frame of a bathroom mirror, and work equally well stuck onto a basket, the delicate blue colors of their insides creating a wonderful watery aura.

SHELL-DECORATED BASKET

Take an old basket whose shape you like – this one has a beautiful handle, whose twists echo those of the shells – and decorate it with a selection of shells stuck on in changing patterns around the outside, the top and just inside the rim. Shell-decorated baskets can look equally good filled with a collection of exotic shells from around the world (as here) or with seasonal fruit or fresh flowers. This basket is the perfect embellishment for a shelf in the bathroom.

Shell Baskets

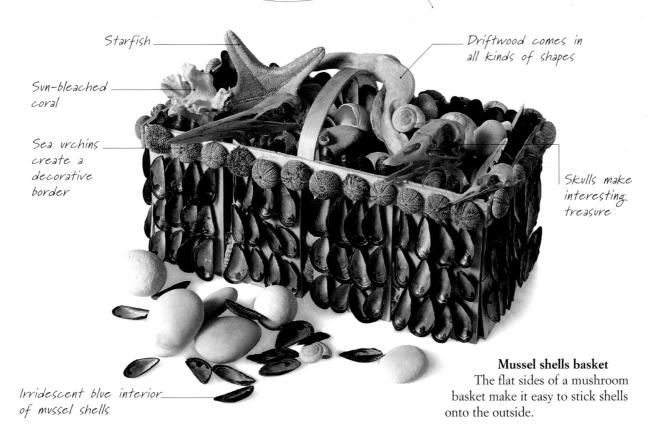

Starfish

Sun-bleached coral

Sea urchins create a decorative border

Driftwood comes in all kinds of shapes

Skulls make interesting treasure

Irridescent blue interior of mussel shells

Mussel shells basket
The flat sides of a mushroom basket make it easy to stick shells onto the outside.

A child's collection
This old mushroom basket (*above*), embellished with mussel shells and sea urchins, houses a child's beachcombing collection.

A pattern of snail shells
A collection of snail shells (*left*) arranged according to their beautiful markings makes a pleasing display.

STICKING ON SEASHELLS
Remove any sand and seaweed from the shells, then rinse and dry them. Place the shells on the floor to work out your pattern (as you might do when threading beads), then stick them onto the basket one at a time, using a strong, instant-bonding glue. Hot glue works well too.

SCENTED LAVENDER

The word lavender comes from the Latin *lavare*, meaning "to wash." Besides using lavender oil as a massage oil to relax muscles before their games, the Romans and Greeks added lavender to their water before bathing. This was a wonderful idea; in addition to its lovely smell, it has a good astringent action, as well as powerful calming properties found in its essential oil form. Its other medicinal uses are as an anti-depressant, and to combat tiredness and nervous headaches.

Lavender has also played an important role in domestic life through the centuries. Insects dislike its strong, sweet smell, so it was strewn among linen to ward off moths and other bugs—with the bonus that it gave the laundry a wonderful fresh scent. In Tudor times, the washing was often spread out on low lavender hedges to dry, again imparting its fragrance to the laundry.

Lavender even has a culinary use. In Elizabethan times it was sprinkled on food, rather like salt and pepper, and made into a conserve. Even now more adventurous cooks experiment by adding some varieties (except the French form, *L. stoechas*, which is poisonous) to salad.

Colors among the many varieties of lavender (more than 25) range from rich blue-purple to delicate shades of pink and white. The flowers also come in different sizes, with the French lavender having the largest flowers.

While many people think of lavender as an essentially Mediterranean herb, conjuring up images of the vast lavender fields of Provence, it is also ubiquitous in country gardens. It was probably brought to England by the Romans, and then its travels continued as it was taken to the New World by the Pilgrims aboard the *Mayflower*.

SUMMER PARTNERS
For a striking color combination and a heavenly mixture of perfumes, combine blowsy English roses with a large bunch of freshly picked lavender and place them in a vibrant basket, securely anchored in a block of well-moistened oasis.

Lavender harvest

In this wonderfully fragrant summer's harvest (*left*), some lavender is gathered in bundles ready for drying (*see page 59*) while the dried stalks await stripping for use in lavender bags. This rustic gardener's basket or "trug" is the perfect shape of basket for laying out the long stems.

Lavender in the bag

Brightly striped material with vivid fuchsia ribbons make these pretty lavender bags a treat to look at, as well as to smell. Place one in a drawer to make your clothes or linen smell wonderfully fresh.

MAKING LAVENDER BAGS

Presentation is as important as perfume, so choose a decorative material for your bags and finish off with a bright ribbon.

1. Strip the dried flowers from a bundle of stems onto paper, then transfer them to a sheet of fabric to conserve every atom of perfume.

2. Place in a warm, dry, airy place until they are thoroughly dry.

3. Sew up small cotton bags on three sides. Put in the dried lavender flowers and tie at the top with a ribbon.

GROWING A LAVENDER PLANT IN A POT

Lavender is a sun-loving shrub that will grow happily in a container.
A small or medium-sized plastic pot can then easily be placed in a
basket—such as this ethnic woven basket from Peru—for a
moveable feast of fragrance.

Plant young lavender in a pot filled with gritty, soil-based potting
mix on top of a drainage layer of broken crockery or pebbles.
Water it regularly and feed occasionally. Trim off the dead flowers
in early autumn and clip it in spring to keep the plant compact. The
lavender can be kept from year to year but will need repotting into
a bigger container in alternate years until it is mature.

Drying lavender
For the best results pick your
lavender early on in its season—
that is, July—and early in the
day, before the sun has had
enough time to evaporate the
volatile oils that give it its
delicious fragrance. If any
drops of dew remain, gently
shake them off. Choose stems
with petals that are just about
to open.

The stems may be spread on a
tray or flat screen to dry, or else
tied in small bunches and hung
upside down (*right*) to prevent
the heads from drooping.
Allow them to dry slowly in an
airy room.

Oil of lavender
Lavender stalks and
flowers are crushed
to extract its essential
oil, often used in
aromatherapy as a
panacea for fatigue
and stress-related
problems.

COOK'S BASKET

As long ago as 3000 B.C. flowers were being used to add color and flavor to cooking. The Chinese first experimented with floral recipes, and they were soon followed in the West by the ancient Greeks, then the Romans. Rose petals, either eaten raw, made into rose water or used simply as decoration, were a great favorite.

But while flowers were popular, herbs were absolutely indispensable. They provided perfume and color, but above all they were valued for their flavorings and their medicinal qualities.

The ancient Greeks discovered the healing power of herbs, and the practice of herbal medicine then spread north through Europe. The Romans brought herbs and knowledge of their use to Britain. During the Dark Ages, all this was lost, but was revived in Norman times by monks traveling from monastery to monastery and taking their expertise with them. Crusaders returning from the Holy Lands also spread knowledge about herbs and their uses.

In Tudor times herbs were plentiful enough to be strewn around houses to sweeten the atmosphere, and were also considered essential in the kitchen. The colonists grew herbs when they settled in the New World. By the eighteenth century every plant and herb was pressed into culinary use—a somewhat risky practice, given the toxic qualities of some herb plants.

While we eat fewer herbs raw today, we still enjoy their scents and flavors and appreciate their qualities. Just think of the bright yellow seedheads of fennel and the beautiful umbrella-shaped flowers of dill, as well as leaves as diverse in shape and texture as those of bay, thyme, marjoram, and sage.

BASKET OF FLAVORS
This basket, brimming with flavored oils, fresh and dried produce and herbs, would delight any cook. Once the herbs are dried they last longer if kept in a dark, dry place, such as this tin container with all its different compartments.

Drying herbs
Dry herbs by spreading them on layers of newspaper or hanging them upside down in a dark, warm place immediately after harvesting. An airy attic is ideal. Turn them regularly and be sure they have plenty of ventilation.

Golden feverfew

Curly-leaved parsley

Common lemon balm

Sweet basil

Chives, from the onion family

One of the many varieties of mint

Dill leaves and flowers

Herb hanging basket
This old tiered vegetable rack (*left*) has been pressed into service of a different sort, for growing herbs. Hung by a French window, the herbs can be protected from too great a draft while enjoying the benefit of plenty of light.

PLANTING AN HERB BASKET

Pack the baskets tightly with tarragon moss, which will form a firm base and hold the moisture in well. Line this with a circle of plastic or aluminum foil to prevent drips, then fill the basket with potting soil. Finally plant up your herbs, choosing a good selection for their looks and scents as well as their flavors. Water when the potting mix is dry and snip them regularly to enhance your cooking.

MAKING HERB OIL

Oil flavored with your own fresh herbs is a real treat and makes a wonderful gift. The bottles will also look spectacular lined up on a shelf—they are too attractive to hide away in a cupboard.

1. Half fill a decorative bottle with sprigs of fresh herbs.
2. Fill up the bottle with olive oil; sunflower oil also works well.
3. Stopper the bottle and leave for two weeks. For stronger flavor, replace the herbs with fresh ones and leave for another two weeks.
4. Strain, leaving just a few sprigs in the bottle for decoration.

AUTUMN

As summer's long days gradually give way to autumn we can find pleasure in the glorious colors this season brings. The russets, golds and fiery reds of the changing leaves are spectacular, and the light takes on a special quality at this time of year, suffused with a beautiful golden hue.

This is harvest time, and as the crops are gathered, we can all—city and country dweller alike—appreciate the bounty of the land and revel in the variety of its produce. The huge range of fruit and dried flowers, cereals and seedheads so plentiful at this time of year look marvelous, yet so natural, arranged in baskets. Such displays look as good in the bedroom as in the living room and they are everlasting.

DOUGH BASKETS

One of the most readily available materials for modeling is salt dough, or sour dough. It is very cheap, since it is made from ingredients that can be found in most kitchens—wonderfully tactile and very simple to sculpt. It is also a truly international modeling material, since flour, water and salt are staple ingredients in most countries' cuisine.

Once kneaded and shaped, this extremely malleable dough can be fired in an ordinary oven, then painted with poster paints or watercolors. It lends itself to being cut into strips and made into a lattice-pattern base or "basket" to hold small objects of any description. The finished dough products look very attractive varnished or, if you want to keep its beautiful golden brown color, they can simply be glazed with egg white.

In Mexico this dough is known as bread glue, and the Mexicans make very intricate, delicate jewelry from it. It is also a key element in their Day of the Dead festivities, when it is made into numerous figures, the most popular being little skeletons, used to decorate the graves of family and friends.

Throughout Central and South America in fact, animals, scenes and characters from everyday life are immortalized in this humble dough. Ecuador has a particularly strong tradition with its ornate bread dolls, while in Peru they make little portable cribs for Christmas, with doors on leather hinges that allow them to open and shut.

ANIMALS OF THE ARK

This spectacular Noah's Ark looks complicated, but is not as difficult to make as it first appears. The boat has a simple lattice base; its sides, roof and ladder are just strands of dough with a little extra decoration and most of the animals are flat cutouts.

The reason this ark and its animal pairs look so professional is the careful and imaginative way they have been finished. The painting is detailed and the colors realistic, with attention paid to texture. A grain has been scratched into the wood and a needle used to make indentations in the sides of the ladder, representing nails, and to define the animals' eyes, mouths and ears.

Dough Baskets

Glossy fresh
vine leaves

Basket of strawberries
Make summer's bounty last well into
autumn with a glazed dough basket
filled with tasty-looking dough fruit.

Twisted-dough rim
to latticework
basket base

Painted
dough leaves

Bunch of grapes
created from
balls of dough

Realistic scarlet
strawberries with tiny
'seed' indentations
picked out in paint

Dough Baskets

Salt Dough

900g (2lb/4 cups) plain flour
225g (8oz/1 cup) salt
450 ml (1 pint) water

1. Mix the flour and salt together, then add the water, stirring vigorously until the ingredients form a ball. This can be done in a food processor.
2. Knead until firm and pliable, with a smooth texture. Any dough not required immediately can be sealed in a plastic bag to prevent it from drying out.
3. Once you have modeled the dough into the desired shape(s), bake in a cool oven, 275–325°F (135–160°C), until hard and dry. Allow 30 minutes for every half a centimeter (¼ inch) of thickness. The hotter the oven temperature, the browner the baked dough.

MAKING A LATTICE BASKET

One of the easiest dough baskets to make is the lattice basket. The trickiest part is the base, which needs to be gently rounded. However, help is at hand in the form of a round breadloaf, which is just the right shape to lay the dough over.

1. Roll the dough flat, then cut it into six (or more) equal-length strips, trimming the ends into a V.
2. Place a loaf on aluminum foil, sprinkle with flour to keep the dough from sticking, then lay the strips over it in a lattice pattern.
3. Bake in a cool oven (*see above left*) until hard, then carefully remove the bread.

Child's dough basket

Let children have fun making and painting dough baskets (*left*). Simply roll the dough into long snakes and plait it to make the base and handle. Paint with poster paints and fill with dough fruit.

AUTUMN HARVEST

Autumn is the time of year when we can sit back and take stock. We have enjoyed the summer, yet we are now ready for a change, and after all the weather isn't yet cold enough to be uncomfortable, or the skies gray enough to be depressing.

It is also a season for taking stock in a more literal sense, for the harvest is being gathered and food supplies laid in. Although those of us who live in towns or cities are far removed from this crop gathering, we can still share the satisfaction of this ritual and some of the traditions associated with it.

Making corn dolls is just such a tradition, and one common throughout the world, from America to India, with Poland and Eastern European countries sharing a particularly strong history of the craft.

Corn is one of the most basic ingredients of all countries' staple foods, whether it be ground to make rough, unleavened bread, the fluffiest French baguette, U.S. cornmeal or Italian polenta. So it is not surprising that the cultivation and harvest of corn figures strongly in many countries'

mythology. In fact, so important were the gods of grain that some pagan cultures even pacified them with human sacrifices.

It was a commonly held belief that the spirit of the corn would retreat as it was harvested, until eventually it was left stranded in the last remaining sheaf. Obviously the cutting of this last sheaf became the focus of various ceremonies and superstitions, and often the sheaf would be preserved, normally in some sort of decorative form. Hence the corn "dolly"—a phrase that also covers numerous forms, from crosses and circles, to rattles and figures.

BASKET OF CORN DOLLIES

This handsome collection of corn dolls in a flat bread basket illustrates a good selection of different styles. There is a simple circle, made up from five-straw plaits, a lovely spiral rattle and, most complex of all, a wreath containing four hearts. The decorative bunches of wheat, oats and barley make an attractive, and particularly apt, backdrop.

Corn-doll angel
Realizing the power of tradition, Christianity cleverly adopted some pagan customs as their own, as this corn-doll angel shows.

Basket of autumn fruits
"Season of mists and mellow fruitfulness..." This sumptuous selection of rich-colored fruit (*left*), with the succulent figs and ripe red plums beside the black grapes, would be perfect for an autumnal picnic.

Golden harvest
Cornflowers, poppies and daisies grow together with cereals in the wild, so it makes perfect sense to display such natural companions together in the home (*below*). The splash of brilliant red and blue brings to life this arrangement in a fruit picker's basket.

MAKING THE CORN-DOLLY PLAIT
The five-straw plait is the basis of all corn dollies. The sides of the octagonal basket above are made of plain straws laid together, using the thickest section, while the rim and the ribs, which hold it all together, are plaited.

1. Strip away any dead material from the straws, then soak them in cold water until flexible (about 15 minutes). Leave upright to drain.
2. Using natural-colored thread, tie the thin ends of five straws around a narrow 40cm (16in) cane.
3. Bend the straws away from the cane at right angles to it, with two pointing north and one straw at each of the other compass points.
4. Bend one north straw over the west straw; bend the west straw over the south and so on.
5. Continue until the straws become too short, then slot the thin ends of five new straws into the plait. Continue until the plait is the right length, then remove the cane.
6. Tie the end of the plait with thread, then leave it soaking in water until it is flexible enough to bend into a circle (about 10 minutes).

THANKSGIVING

The festival of Thanksgiving is a day set aside to celebrate the bravery of America's founders, to remember the hardships they endured, and to look with gratitude upon what the current year has brought. It is also a wonderful family occasion, and an excuse for loved ones scattered all over the country to gather together.

As Thanksgiving falls on the fourth Thursday of November, it also doubles as an opportunity to give thanks for the harvest. This is traditionally the time of year when storage cupboards should be groaning. It is the season of plenty before the exigencies of winter.

Autumn is drawing to a close, and many of the leaves are still on the trees. The predominant colors of this glorious display are gentle reds and flaming golds. In New England, where the trees are at their most magnificent, makeshift stands laden with enormous, fantastically colored squashes, often called gourds, line the roadsides.

The flesh of many of these squashes can be cooked—pumpkin pie being the best-known dish and the traditional dessert at Thanksgiving dinner—but some are used simply for decoration, or they may be hollowed out to make jack-o'-lanterns for the Hallowen celebrations.

Maize, another important crop in the United States, was one of the earliest to be cultivated. Like the gourds, maize can be very colorful, ranging from bright yellow to shades of deep reddish-brown and purplish-black, and therefore makes a brilliant display in a Thanksgiving basket.

SEASON OF PLENTY

This typical American harvest looks quite at home in a Mediterranean basket. The long, tapering maize ears contrast prettily with the full roundness of the gourds. This arrangement demonstrates that vegetables can be just as attractive and decorative as flowers. When put beside flowers, such as these sunflowers and Chinese lanterns, the effect of the rich combination of colors is quite spectacular.

Basket of maize

Even before the first settlers set foot on American soil, maize was being cultivated by some Native American tribes. After the harvest a few heads were always saved for decoration. The brown leather-covered handle and the red and yellow coloring of this basket blend well with the colors of the maize.

Dried oranges

This garden basket houses a seasonal collection of cut, dried oranges. The dark ivy leaves provide good contrast to the fruit. Twined prettily around the handle, they make it more suitable for use indoors.

Shallow sides are designed to hold cut flowers

Ivy leaves twined around handle

Cut slices of dried orange

Gardener's basket

Basket of gourds
Gourds come in an astonishing range of colors, patterns and shapes, from the flattish butternut squash to the better-known orange pumpkin.

CUTTING ORANGES FOR DRYING

1. Using a very sharp knife, cut about eight slim wedge-shaped indentations into the orange.
2. Peel away the wedge-shaped pieces of skin to reveal the darker flesh beneath.
3. Leave the orange in a warm, dry place for a few weeks. As it dries, the orange will shrink slightly and the cuts will look more pronounced, contrasting with the flesh inside.

DRIED FLOWERS

During autumn and winter when there are fewer fresh flowers around, dried flowers and seedheads come into their own. They can brighten up awkward spaces and they look stunning mixed with fresh material. They can also effectively tone down rather too brightly colored fresh flowers, rescuing a floral arrangement that might otherwise look too harsh. At the start of this century all design, floral included, underwent a revolution, with a move away from rigidity and formality towards a new minimalism. At this time Charles Rennie Mackintosh was using bowlfuls of colored twigs for decoration, and seedheads—which would previously have been discarded—were kept to be used in simple arrangements.

Now it is accepted that nuts, vegetables, wheat, thistles and pinecones, as well as interestingly shaped twigs (tortured willow being very popular) can all be used to make beautiful creations. Even artificial flowers, long seen as the poor relation to fresh and dried, should not be dismissed out of hand. These have always been considered by some to be bad taste—possibly because the word *artificial* conjures up visions of garish plastic daffodils and chrysanthemums—but now, with the advent of delicate paper or fabric (often silk) flowers, they can be just as attractive as the real thing.

Always buy the best you can afford—the more expensive they are, the less likely they are to fade—and try to match the flowers to the season. There is something extremely disconcerting about seeing poinsettias in midsummer.

EVERLASTING FLOWER BASKET
This elegant arrangement cleverly mixes dried flowers and seedheads with artificial material, yet it is virtually impossible to spot what is not real. The warm, muted colors seem to glow with the ghost of summer sun while still being the very essence of autumn. The sculptural-looking seedheads of poppies and thistles promise blooms to come, while the roses provide a permanent reminder of past joys.

Everlasting flowers

Everlasting flowers—statice and strawflowers, also known as immortelles—have been prized through the centuries for their long-lasting qualities and the fact that they do not change much when dried. Without them there would have been no flowers at all indoors during the long dark winter months.

This garlanded basket (*left*) is a celebration of a bountiful harvest. The roundness and solidity of the fruit contrast with and highlight the papery delicacy and fragility of these everlasting flowers.

Miniature flower baskets

Miniature baskets can be arranged in groups of complementary or contrasting colors and also look appealing on their own. If kept out of the sun their colors will not fade and, as long as you blow any dust away occasionally, they will look this good all winter.

The seedheads of love-in-a-mist (*right*) have a striped appearance that looks charming when the heads are massed together.

The dried flower-heads of yarrow (*left*) form a lovely small yellow globe when displayed in a miniature basket.

THREADING DRIED FLOWERS

Everlasting flowers make a wonderful garland for a basket handle. You will find it easier to decorate the main body of the basket before decorating the handle.

1. Sort out bunches of about six flowers and bind with tape or wire just below the flowerhead.
2. Working from left to right, lay your first bunch against the handle with the stems to the right, then bind the stems to the handle with fine florist's wire.
3. Place the next bunch so that the flowerheads conceal the stems of the previous bunch and repeat until the handle is almost covered.
4. Lay the final bunch the opposite way, so its stems hide under the previous flowerheads. To attach the flowers to the sides of the basket, bind them in small bunches as before but leave long lengths of wire spare. Next cut the stems as short as possible and place the bunches against the sides of the basket. Feed the wires through the wicker and twist on the inside.

Seedheads collection

The exuberant display (*right*) looks especially spectacular in this woven rattan basket. The combination of the Oriental basket and the wild profusion of seedheads, which are somehow the essence of autumn in the Western Hemisphere, is particularly irresistible.

The muted golds and browns of this collection gives it a glowing quality. Although the individual elements are humble, grouped together they look spectacular. The different textures and shapes—rough, spiky, fluffy and smooth—are endlessly fascinating, drawing the eye and giving this basket an enduring fascination.

Children will love playing at being squirrels and collecting seedheads such as these. It is worth taking a bag with you on walks in a woodland to carry any finds, while the more exotic seedheads can be bought at a good florist or garden center.

Mixed miniature posy

This is a posy for all seasons. The spiky eryngiums (thistles) look particularly striking and evoke a feeling of summer, while the dried poppy seedheads look very autumnal. Other dried flowers used in this attractively colored miniature basket include those with delicate-looking flowerheads, such as sea lavender, gypsophila, silvery honesty and straw or everlasting flowers. They are punctuated with slim, elongated gray-green eucalyptus leaves. The stems are anchored in a block of oasis cut to the shape of the basket (*see page 38*).

Using silk flowers

Mixing artificial and dried flowers can produce excellent results (*left*). These silk roses are especially attractive, looking as full-blown and floppy as any variety of old English rose. Silk is the ideal material for making roses as its sheen matches perfectly the velvety quality of real rose petals.

Dried Flowers

Dried
seaweed

Dried daisy-
like flowers

Spiky
artichokes

Poppyheads

Split
seedpods

Rattan
basket

WINTER

As the evenings shorten and we retreat inside, there are numerous consolations, not least the excitement of the December holidays. Early winter is a time of planning and preparation. Family festivals offer the excuse to splash out on decorating the house. It is also a great time to reorganize sewing and craft supplies for winter projects.

A beautiful basket filled with holly, ivy or pinecones creates an atmosphere of opulence. It is fun to bring as much as we can of the outdoors in, since we rarely venture out in this season. For most of us, the chance to gather around a blazing fire or holiday banquet is an infinitely more alluring prospect.

WORK BASKETS

Baskets are the ideal storage place for the needlework or crafts that occupy long wintry evenings by the fireside. They come in so many different shapes that it is not hard to find one that suits your particular requirements, whether it be balls of yarn or spools of silk. If you need to carry your work basket around, choose a basket with a deep handle, such as the shopping basket opposite. However, a shallower basket is more appropriate for trinkets or jewelry.

There is something immensely satisfying about a well-ordered work basket. If yours is constantly on show, put in a little effort to ensure that it always looks presentable. Choose a pretty material for the lining and stitch compartments into it so that it looks neat at all times.

Making a lining

The lining is made up of three sections: one follows the shape of the base, while two long strips make up the sides.

1. To line the bottom, trace the base of the basket onto the fabric and cut it out. Turn the edges under and stitch.

2. To line the sides, measure the circumference of the basket and cut two strips of fabric to that length, one as deep as the basket plus 5cm (2in) for seam allowance, the other about 2.5cm (1in) narrower. Turn under and stitch along one long edge of each strip. Lay them flat, right sides up, with the narrower strip on top. They should be even along the unturned long edge, which will be the bottom. Tack the two bottom edges together. To form the pockets, tack the strips together vertically at regular intervals. Then sew the short edges together to form a circle.

3. Place the lining in the basket and tack the wider strip to the basket edge.

SEWING BASKET

There is no risk of a muddle with this customized shopping basket designed to hold sewing equipment (*right*). The pockets in the lining keep each spool of thread separate, leaving space in the center for pin cushion, needlecase, scissors, buttons and rolls of ribbon or tape. The tall handle makes it easy to carry.

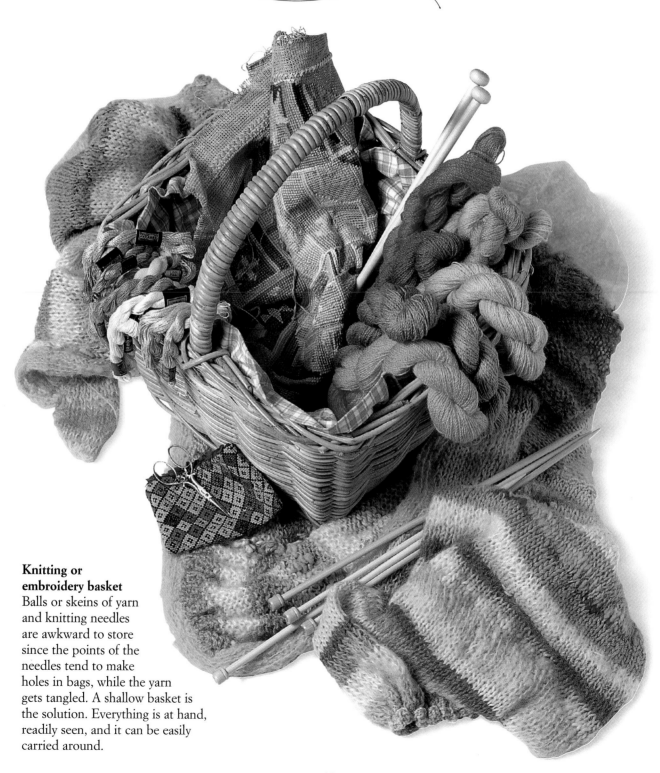

Knitting or embroidery basket
Balls or skeins of yarn and knitting needles are awkward to store since the points of the needles tend to make holes in bags, while the yarn gets tangled. A shallow basket is the solution. Everything is at hand, readily seen, and it can be easily carried around.

Work bag

Make a bag-cum-basket (*right*) to keep silks and threads separate and to hold any sewing work in progress. The drawstring will keep any fabric clean and it doubles as a handle.

Basket of beads

A shallow rattan basket with a compartmentalized fabric lining is perfect for storing beads, as they are easy to get at and easy to see. This is ideal if you make your own necklaces, earrings or other jewelry. The ethnic look of this rattan basket suits the chunky beads, while the soft fabric lining helps to prevent scratches.

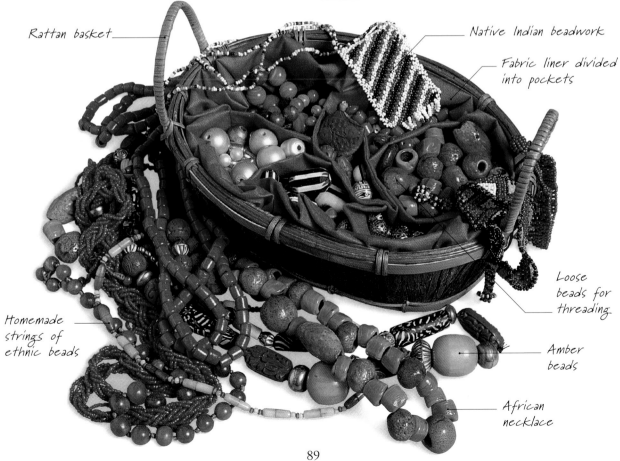

Rattan basket

Native Indian beadwork

Fabric liner divided into pockets

Loose beads for threading

Homemade strings of ethnic beads

Amber beads

African necklace

CHRISTMAS BASKETS

Even the most jaded adult will feel a flicker of excitement as Christmas approaches. For children, it is a time of glorious wonderment, almost unbearable excitement and glitter.

The traditional colors of Christmas—red, green, golden-yellow and white—reflect the plants and the weather. The greens and reds are those of ivy and holly laden with berries, the white of snow and the delicate hellebores and early narcissi. Now, of course, the choice has widened with the availability of more exotic blooms, such as poinsettias and forced hyacinths (with their heady perfumes, the strength of which is only matched by their vivid colors—blue, pink and white).

We traditionally decorate our homes for Christmas using candles and ornaments in these colors, besides natural materials such as fir cones and fruit. Nothing is as evocative as the smell of wood fires and the resiny scent of Christmas trees and pinecones. To complement the colors and perfumes, candles create a wonderfully Christmasy atmosphere. Their light is intimate, yet welcoming.

In many regions of Eastern Europe it is traditional to place a lit candle at a window on Christmas Eve as a sign of hospitality and to help travelers along their way—a custom said to hark back to the way the Christmas star guided the three Wise Men. Candlelight is elegant and extremely flattering at the same time, and the tall shapes of the candles, combined with flowers, foliage, tree ornaments, ribbons and bells, are very decorative. For a Christmas variation on the theme of pot-et-fleurs, combine a red candle with a potted hyacinth or fresh narcissi in a basket, perhaps for a visitor's bedroom.

SEASONAL MANTELPIECE

This unusual arrangement of small baskets is North European in origin. The candles, berries, hips and ivy, along with the crackers and presents, give the mantelpiece a very festive appearance. It would be fun to light a candle for each member of the family and each guest, or even to represent each of the twelve days of Christmas by a candle.

Floating candles

A basket filled with floating candles (*left*) looks glorious on a table. The bobbing motion of the candles and their flickering light is mesmerizing, and mixed with the green of the ivy and the gold of the foil-covered chocolates will add a special touch of magic to a Christmas table.

Ivy threaded through the sides of a plastic-lined basket will disguise and soften the rim, as well as hiding the shallow glass bowl of water in which the candles float. A few dainty narcissi flowers floating alongside the candles and chocolates will release a heavenly scent.

Basket of crackers

Homemade or store-bought "crackers" are a long-standing English tradition. The homemade variety can be filled with gifts to suit each guest's tastes.

MAKING POMANDERS

1. Choose a ripe, thin-skinned orange—preferably Seville—and bind it tightly with a circle of narrow masking tape or a broad rubber band.
2. Using a skewer or fine knitting needle, pierce the skin and insert one clove at a time until the orange is covered. Follow the edges of the tape carefully to ensure the cloves are in neat lines.
3. Once the orange is covered with cloves, put it in a paper bag with a mixure of equal parts powdered orris root and cinnamon (ground nutmeg and allspice may also be added), allowing about a teaspoon of each per orange. Shake until it is completely covered.
4. Wrap the bag, orange and all, in tissue paper and leave in a dry place for two or three weeks. Then peel off the tape before putting the pomander back in the bag for another couple of weeks.
5. Once it has dried out, decorate with ribbon, leaving a long length for a loop at the top.

The origin of pomanders

The word pomander comes from the French *pomme d'ambre*—meaning apple of amber; however, pomanders were originally perforated balls of china, silver or gold. These were filled with potpourri (dried herbs or spices), and in medieval times they were carried around by people to ward off infection. Orange pomanders—the cheaper, everyday version of these treasures—will perfume a room with their pungent aroma. Otherwise they can be placed in a wardrobe or in drawers, where their spicy fragrance will last even longer.

Pomander basket

This unusual star-shaped basket (*right*) is perfect for the Christmas season. The fragrant, spicily scented pomanders, with their glossy ribbons, are grouped together in a basket for maximum impact. They also look lovely hanging on the Christmas tree.

INDEX OF BASKET PROJECTS